Mom & Son Journal Teens & Tweens Edition
By: Iona Yeung

© Copyright 2018 - All rights reserved.

The contents of this book may not be reproduced, duplicated or transmitted without direct written permission from the author.

Under no circumstances will any legal responsibility or blame be held against the publisher for any reparation, damages, or monetary loss due to the information herein, either directly or indirectly.

Legal Notice:

This book is copyright protected. This is only for personal use. You cannot amend, distribute, sell, use, quote or paraphrase any part or the content of this book without the consent of the author.

Disclaimer Notice:

Please note the information contained in this document is for educational and entertainment purposes only. Every attempt has been made to provide accurate, up to date and reliable, complete information. No warranties of any kind are expressed or implied. Readers acknowledge that the author is not engaging in the rendering of legal, financial, medical or professional advice. The content of this book has been derived from various sources. Please consult a licensed professional before attempting any techniques outlined in this book.

By reading this document, the reader agrees that under no circumstances are is the author responsible for any losses, direct or indirect, which are incurred as a result of the use of information contained within this document, including, but not limited to, — errors, omissions, or inaccuracies.

Why journal?

These journal prompts are designed to strengthen the bond between a mother and son, to uncover things you may not know about each other before.

Because sometimes it's easier to put thoughts onto paper.
Take the time to reflect, ask questions, doodle, scribble.

Use this as a tool to have deeper discussions.

To my son,
What I love about you...

_____

_____

_____

_____

_____

_____

_____

_____

_____

_____

_____

_____

_____

_____

_____

To my mom,
What I love about you...

_____

_____

_____

_____

_____

_____

_____

_____

_____

_____

_____

_____

To my son,
What is your idea of the perfect day?

To my mom,
What is your idea of the perfect day?

_____
_____
_____
_____
_____
_____
_____
_____
_____
_____
_____
_____
_____
_____
_____

To my son,
When was the last time you felt really loved?

To my mom,
When was the last time you felt really loved?

_____

_____

_____

_____

_____

_____

_____

_____

_____

_____

_____

_____

To my son,
What's something you've always wanted to ask me?

___
___
___
___
___
___
___
___
___
___
___
___
___
___
___

To my mom,
What's something you've always wanted to ask me?

_____

_____

_____

_____

_____

_____

_____

_____

_____

_____

_____

_____

_____

_____

To my son,
What's the scariest thing you've done?

To my son,
What's the scariest thing you've done?

To my son,
What's one thing you don't often tell your friends?

To my mom,
What's one thing you don't often tell your friends?

To my son,
If you could quite school/work and do whatever you want, what would you want to do?

_____
_____
_____
_____
_____
_____
_____
_____
_____
_____
_____
_____

To my mom,
If you could quite school/work and do whatever you want, what would you want to do?

_____
_____
_____
_____
_____
_____
_____
_____
_____
_____
_____
_____

To my son,
What do you admire in people your age?

To my mom,
What do you admire in people your age?

_____
_____
_____
_____
_____
_____
_____
_____
_____
_____
_____
_____
_____

To my son,
What's something you'd like for us to do together?

_____

_____

_____

_____

_____

_____

_____

_____

_____

_____

_____

To my mom,
What's something you'd like for us to do together?

___
___
___
___
___
___
___
___
___
___
___
___
___
___

To my son, what does your life look like in 5 years? Doodle it.

To my mom, what does your life look like in 5 years? Doodle it.

To my son,
What's one thing you've always wanted to tell me?

To my mom,
What's one thing you've always wanted to tell me?

To my son, do you see the glass full or empty?

Yes/No

To my mom, do you see the glass full or empty?

Yes/No

To my son,
If you could eat one meal for the rest of your life, which would it be?

_____
_____
_____
_____
_____
_____
_____
_____
_____
_____
_____
_____

To my mom,
If you could eat one meal for the rest of your life, which would it be?

_____

_____

_____

_____

_____

_____

_____

_____

_____

_____

_____

_____

_____

To my son,
Do you believe in love at first sight?

To my mom,
Do you believe in love at first sight?

___
___
___
___
___
___
___
___
___
___
___
___
___

To my son,
If you were to learn something new, what would it be?

_____

_____

_____

_____

_____

_____

_____

_____

_____

_____

_____

_____

To my mom,
If you were to learn something new, what would it be?

___

___

___

___

___

___

___

___

___

___

___

___

To my son,
Do you have a secret talent?

_____

_____

_____

_____

_____

_____

_____

_____

_____

_____

_____

To my mom,
Do you have a secret talent?

_____

_____

_____

_____

_____

_____

_____

_____

_____

_____

_____

_____

To my son,
If the world were to end tomorrow, what would you do today?

To my mom,
If the world were to end tomorrow, what would you do today?

___

To my son,
What's one song you can listen to over and over again?

To my mom,
What's one song you can listen to over and over again?

To my son,
What's one movie you can watch over and over again?

To my mom,
What's one movie you can watch over and over again?

___
___
___
___
___
___
___
___
___
___
___
___
___
___

To my son,
If you could be a super hero for the day, which one would you be?

_____
_____
_____
_____
_____
_____
_____
_____
_____
_____
_____
_____
_____
_____

To my mom,
If you could be a super hero for the day, which one would you be?

_____

_____

_____

_____

_____

_____

_____

_____

_____

_____

_____

_____

To my son,
What's something that makes you sad?

To my mom,
What's something that makes you sad?

To my son,
What's something that always makes you happy?

To my mom,
What's something that always makes you happy?

_____

_____

_____

_____

_____

_____

_____

_____

_____

_____

_____

_____

To my son,
What's something that always makes you sad?

___

To my mom,
What's something that always makes you sad?

To my son,
What should I do to cheer you up when you're sad?

___
___
___
___
___
___
___
___
___
___
___
___

To my mom,
What should I do to cheer you up when you're sad?

___
___
___
___
___
___
___
___
___
___
___
___
___

To my son,
What's one thing you enjoy doing together?

___
___
___
___
___
___
___
___
___
___
___
___
___
___
___
___

To my mom,
What's one thing you enjoy doing together?

___
___
___
___
___
___
___
___
___
___
___
___

To my son,
What's on your bucket list?

To my mom,
What's on your bucket list?

To my son,
What can I do to get to know you better?

To my mom,
What can I do to get to know you better?

To my son, let's play a game

Let's play again

Best 2 out of 3?

To my son, this is what my perfect day looks like in drawing...

To my mom, this is what my perfect day looks like in drawing...

Things for us to share

Our joint bucket list

A list of movies we can watch together

_____

_____

_____

_____

_____

_____

_____

_____

_____

_____

_____

_____

A list of books we can read and discuss

Things to do together this year

Letters

One for every month of the year

Letters to my son

Letters to my son

Letters to my son

Letters to my son

Letters to my son

Letters to my son

Letters to my son

Letters to my son

Letters to my son

Letters to my son

Letters to my son

Letters to my son

Letters to my mom

Letters to my mom

Letters to my mom

Letters to my mom

Letters to my mom

Letters to my mom

_____
_____
_____
_____
_____
_____
_____
_____
_____
_____
_____
_____

Letters to my mom

Letters to my mom

Letters to my mom

Letters to my mom

Notes & Doodles

Use this to unleash your creativity, play a game of hangman or jot down ideas to discuss

Made in the USA
Middletown, DE
08 December 2024

66367275R00056